ORIENT

ORIENT

*Two Walks at the Edge
of the Human*

DAVID HINTON

SHAMBHALA

Shambhala Publications, Inc.
2129 13th Street
Boulder, Colorado 80302
www.shambhala.com

Grateful acknowledgment is made to *Emergence Magazine*,
in whose pages selections of this book first appeared.

Cover art: "Grand Canyon" by Clare Romano
Cover design: Daniel Urban-Brown and Meredith Jarrett

Interior design: Steve Dyer

9 8 7 6 5 4 3 2 1

FIRST EDITION
Printed in the United States of America

Shambhala Publications makes every effort
to print on acid-free, recycled paper.
Shambhala Publications is distributed worldwide by
Penguin Random House, Inc., and its subsidiaries.

LIBRARY OF CONGRESS CATALOGING-IN-PUBLICATION DATA
Names: Hinton, David, 1954– author.
Title: Orient: two walks at the edge of the human / David Hinton.
Description: First edition. | Boulder, Colorado: Shambhala, [2025]
Identifiers: LCCN 2024025505 | ISBN 9781645472759 (trade paperback)
Subjects: LCSH: Taoism.
Classification: LCC BL1900.A2 H56 2025 | DDC 299.5/14—dc23/
eng/20240916
LC record available at https://lccn.loc.gov/2024025505

The authorized representative in the EU for product safety and
compliance is eucomply OÜ, Pärnu mnt 139b-14, 11317 Tallinn, Estonia,
hello@eucompliancepartner.com.

CONTENTS

v

ORIENT

INTRODUCTION

(Breath-Space and Seed-Time)

I T WAS WONDROUS ENOUGH AS COYOTE'S mischief, or Sun and Moon losing themselves in the dark love-making of solar eclipse. But in empirical fact, the birthplace of stars is now always everywhere, a quantum particle-burst blossoming out and flaring starlight where the mysterious fabric of gravity tightens. The more we know about it, the more wondrous it becomes, and we can see through knowing to the question that remains: Being, shadowy Being somehow ablaze with itself here, even after thinning and cooling for nearly fifteen billion years.

This is the Cosmos that modern science describes as *space-time*, a mysterious gravity-flexed fabric of continents and oceans, stars and galaxies, black holes and dark matter. *Space-time* is an uncannily literal translation of 宇宙, one of ancient China's foundational cosmological concepts. There are similarities between the two concepts, and 宇宙 too seems empirically accurate, but it is also something more, something primordial and alive and portrayed clearly in the pictographic dimensions of its ideograms (still visible in their current standardized forms: 宇宙).

宇 portrays breath spreading beneath a roof: 𠆢, end-view of a traditional Chinese roof, its dragon-spine ridge and wing-curve slope. Hence: "the space beneath eaves" or "house." Then by extension, it comes to mean "breath spreading free beneath the canopy of heaven," from which is derived "the space beneath the canopy of heaven," and on to "space," "space itself as dwelling-place," dwelling-place alive with primal breath. And so, the Cosmos as a living breath-infused expanse, as our *breath-space* home.

Similarly, 宙 depicts a seed sprouting beneath that same dragon-spine and wing-curve roof, from which comes the meaning "home" or "dwelling-place." By extension, this becomes "a seed burgeoning forth beneath the canopy of heaven," which comes to mean "time," "time itself as dwelling-place." And this seed is also infused with that primal breath, making it the very image of a more primordial understanding of time as an all-encompassing present, a constant burgeoning forth to which we belong wholly. And so, the Cosmos as a generative self-emergent tissue, as our *seed-time* home.

Combined, 气 and 曲 describe the two dimensions that weave together to form this Cosmos as a tissue of breath-emergent transformation. And another foundational concept from ancient China describes this emergence as 自然 (*tzu-jan*), meaning "occurrence appearing of itself": the ten thousand things burgeoning forth spontaneously from the generative source, each according to its own nature, independent and self-sufficient, each dying and returning to the process of change, only to reappear in another form. Vast and deep, everything and everywhere, including all the depths of our mental realm, this *breath-seed* occurrence is always moving and changing. It is alive somehow—existence-tissue magically, mysteriously, inexplicably alive. It is whole—but not complete, never complete. Instead, it is pregnant through and through, subjective and objective realms a single generative tissue all dynamic energy in perpetual transformation: the Cosmos my ancient Chinese teachers inhabited with an awesome sense of wonder and the sacred.

We know time and space as grand cosmic dimensions that function as unthought and even unnoticed assumptions: linear time a metaphysical river coursing past us as future flows through present into past; abstract space a metaphysical void within which the physical objects of our actual world reside and move and interact. These assumptions about the world structure our immediate experience, locating us outside the fundamental movement of natural process, the elemental reality of the Cosmos. But these unnoticed and unthought dimensions of time and space that we take so for granted—if we look for them in the actual fabric of reality, we cannot find them. Instead, we find only occurrence itself. Time is an ongoing and all-encompassing generative moment, a constant burgeoning forth of occurrence: the ten thousand things each emerging, for a moment, then vanishing away. And space is simply those ten thousand things themselves, the dimensional array of occurrence that we inhabit with absolute immediacy. Space as 宇 and time as 宙: *breath-space* and *seed-time*, ongoing occurrence itself as our dwelling-place, our *breath-seed home*.

Wanting to see through all those unnoticed assumptions and reinhabit this *breath-seed home* fully, I walk out through desert distances to a village abandoned over a thousand years ago and now fallen into ruins. It's exquisite: a place that, precisely because it is so empty and inhospitable, offers the possibility of *dwelling*. There's almost nothing left of the culture that once thrived here: a few remnant walls, carefully laid stone mostly tumbled and scattered back into desert. Almost nothing, but enough to reveal how those walls were oriented to the movement of sun and moon and stars. And calendars remain, still marking solstices: rock casting a light-line on rock-etched spiral, petroglyph face with eyes lit by the precise angle of sun. That's when I come: two walks, one at each of the year's two solstice moments, summer and winter, moments revealing the apex of brightness and darkness, fullness and emptiness, life and death. Moments that also reveal that 宗 曲 cosmology.

Ruins remain, calendars remain, and that cosmology too remains. The anthropologist Benjamin Lee Whorf discovered it in deep strata of the language this landscape's ancient culture handed down. Instead of our space and time, he discovered a foundational assumption that the ongoing transformation of reality, both mental and physical, is a perpetual process of breath-driven emergence from a seed of emptiness that

exists in the mind, or as the Hopi would prefer to say, in the heart, not only the heart of man [sic], but in the heart of animals, plants, and things, and behind and within all the forms and appearances of nature in the heart of nature, and by an implication and extension which has been felt by more than one anthropologist, yet would hardly ever be

> *spoken of by a Hopi himself, so charged is the idea with religious and magical awesomeness, in the very heart of the Cosmos itself.**

Remarkably, Whorf's account of Hopi language embodying that primal cosmology also describes the deep structure of classical Chinese perfectly. Rather than verb tenses inscribing our metaphysics of linear time into consciousness, classical Chinese verbs are unconjugated, simply registering emergence, occurrence appearing of itself in a kind of boundless present. And classical Chinese has minimal grammar, so pictographic ideograms seem to be each emerging from a generative emptiness. There are many more examples, and taken together they form the deep structure of classical Chinese. Hence, that 宇宙 cosmology as an unthought assumption shaping the minds of my ancient teachers: reality seen as a generative tissue—as female, mother.

The pictographic images in 宇宙 are one way ancient China described this living Cosmos. Another is dragon, the mythic embodiment of that shadowy starlit Being. Feared and revered as the venerable

---

* Benjamin Lee Whorf, "An American Indian Model of the Universe," in *Language, Thought, and Reality: Selected Writings* (Cambridge, MA: Technology Press of Massachusetts Institute of Technology, 1956), 59–60.

force of change, dragon is in constant transformation, writing through all creation and destruction, all appearance and disappearance, shaping itself into the ten thousand things soaring through their traceless transformations, their origins and vanishings. This was seen as a kind of magisterial flight, captured in the ideogram for "dragon," in which the image of a dragon's body (𩖮) is graced with wings (𦐇): 龍.

Alive with dragon-spine and wing-curve, this 冂囲 Cosmos is dragon's realm, is indeed dragon itself. And according to ancient Chinese legend, we are ourselves descended from dragons: Root-Breath and Lady She-Voice. Not long after primordial chaos separated into heaven and earth, Root-Breath and Lady She-Voice emerged half-dragon and half-human from Bright-Distance Mountain. They were the original couple, and Lady She-Voice gave birth to the first humans. So, we have dragon hearts pumping dragon blood, dragon minds thinking dragon thoughts. And our eyes, too, our unfathomable eyes that can see through knowing to the question that remains: we look with dragon-deep eyes, as the oracle-bone ideogram for "eye" suggests: 𤇆. And it all begins with those eyes. That's why I set out on these solstice walks: wide-open desert returns me to dragon-deep eyes gazing into dragon, into this 冂囲 dwelling-place, this *breath-seed home.*

WALK ONE

(Breath-Space)

Desert

Sky

Sagebrush

Sun

Ruins

Wasp

SIGHT! HOW WONDROUS: THAT THE WORLD
is open inside me, all this light and space somehow
mirrored wide-open inside me: desert, sky, sagebrush,
sun, ruins, wasp! Sight, dragon-eye sight!

Cottonwood

Sun-Quick Lizard

Experience defines us. It makes us what we are. Places wandered and people known, books read and ideas pursued, the events of our lives: experience is narrative, history, story. What books are normally about. Story is how we define ourselves as human, how we know ourselves. And the singular stories of our lives make us each unique individuals. So it makes sense that people are interested in experience. And sight in and of itself is so altogether immediate and empty that there seems nothing to notice, nothing to think through and understand. But it's miraculous, all this light and space mirrored wide-open inside us. Miraculous and fundamental, something prior to the definitions of experience and story, something we are more entirely even than we are ourselves. Looking for the least possible definition and story, for sight's most expansive emptiness and all the ravishing depths it reveals, I set out into horizon-wide desert, follow a sunbaked trail across dry washes and uplands (rattlesnake keeping cool in piñon shade), passing petroglyphs of bighorn sheep and cougar, moon and stars etched on clean sandstone walls beneath the mud nests of cliff swallows that enliven the air with their sleek flight. Occasional lightning-haunted clouds and sprinkles of rain drift in blue skies. And when I reach the village, I begin wandering desert distances and ancient ruins, wall-stones tumbled and scattered—the edge where the last remnant of human self-definition is feathering away into everything else. It's bewildering. What am I this empty and mirror-deep? And where am I amid these desert distances outside stretching away inside? It's summer solstice, day long with light and all its clarities. I wander, and soon begin gathering stones one by one. I settle stone beside stone on earth, laying a foundation, beginning to build a small cairn, to orient.

Circling Hawk (Red-

Tail Sun-Flash)

Deadwood Shadow-Twist

Call it Cosmos or shadowy Being, 宂甶 or dragon, the tissue of existence in its elemental molecular structure is opaque. And so, the eye is truly miraculous. Little waterpocket-fold all empty clarity, it's a site where the utter opacity of matter is somehow open to itself, mirroring itself. The eye: at the very heart of things is the eye. The ideogram for *sincerity* is 信, its pictographic elements portraying a person standing by words: 亻 (modified form of 人, side view of a person walking) beside 言 (image of words rising out of a mouth). It implies that if we are sincere, our thoughts cleave true to our words: inner true to outer. And by extension, *sincerity* becomes "thoughts true to actions": again, inner true to outer. This suggests *sincerity* most fundamentally describes an identification of outside and inside. And indeed, the English word's etymology traces back to the Latin *sincerus*, meaning "whole, pure, one growth." Sight is an elemental form of this sincerity— for in mirrored sight, inside is precisely outside, and outside inside. And in this sincerity, all these depths of the world opening inside me, I am altogether true and kindred to the ten thousand things of this world. What great good fortune! Here in this desert empty of story and definition, there is no difference anywhere between myself and the horizon-wide breath-space of these desert distances. Free of myself, sight caressing things—edges and textures, forms and colors and distances—the eye alive at the very heart of things: it's like nothing so much as flight, light-drenched flight.

Basalt Lichen-Stained (Orange)

Sky-Lit Sky

There's almost nothing left, nothing of the village that once thrived here. Only a few remnants of wall remain, more absent than present. All that carefully laid stone, shelter mostly emptied away into ruins tumbled back to earth and scattered across desert: it's the edge where human order sifts away into everything else. And it's the perfect place to forget what I am and everything that defines me—all the experiences and ideas, stories and assumptions. Forgetting and forgetting, I return to sight in and of itself. I wander at the edge of the human here in these ruins, at the beginning of the human—before even the earliest story and art, idea and explanation. All of that must have begun in some primordial act of orientation: a first cairn, perhaps. A few stones piled tentatively up, that first cairn began to define a place, a human place in relation to everything around it.

Rain(Desert)Gust

Pumice-Grit Earth

Fritillary

Forgetting and forgetting, it's easy to return to the clarity of that first cairn. I carry a few more ruinstones, nestle them onto those foundation stones:

one over two, two over one. And it begins to orient, this first-cairn of mine. It begins to mean everything around it, for where does it end? Its extent includes all of this desert landscape, this topography. When we speak of things, when we name them, they become objects in an elsewhere somehow separate from us. But a cairn says nothing, creates no elsewhere. It keeps things whole, like sight. I pile a few ruin-stones slowly. Here at the beginning, keeping things whole, I orient:

Ridgeline Snow-Distances

Apache-Plume (Red Thread-

Wander Fluff)

How exquisite when things fall apart: no idea who I am, no idea where. Ruins. Ruins mirror-deep, opening such emptiness: empty mind, empty sight, empty life-time. Suddenly, the moon lofts huge over a mesa-rim horizon here in this emptiness. Midday heat ripples air. Wind whispers through, late light slants through, stars wheel through this emptiness. Days and nights and whole lifetimes stream through unscathed and empty, empty.

Ocotillo Spire-Wander

Piñon Cone-Scatter

Petroglyph Wings

I gather a few more stones, settle them next to each other, on top of each other. Mute and elemental, a cairn orients, marks the way. It says nothing, nothing about the landscape it orients around itself: distances of desert and mountain. It orients, and yet remains empty, for it is about everything other than itself. Sincerity: whole, pure, one growth, inside exactly outside and outside inside. This self we each are in our everyday routine, this "I" here in the grammar: it creates the illusion that I inhabit an isolate interiority, that sight is a kind of inside looking out to an outside. It's lonely, that breach between me and everything else. But here in the actual moment of seeing, it's all sincerity. I can't find that self I am anywhere, that inside we assume looks out to an outside. And I can't find that loneliness. What I find instead is simply awareness open to the world, awareness like a mirror filled with the world: no self, no subject, no inside. It's the same sincerity that this little cairn conjures, and it opens me to 宇, desert's breath-space distances stretching away. Cairn and sight: they seem perfect, seem complete and still and whole celebrating existence itself, the depths of sheer existence. These depths open their distances mirror-deep through me, and I am nowhere right here where they open, nowhere and beginning to orient, orient:

Yellow Bud-Haze Chamisa

Boulder-Scree (Tumble-Black)

Existence. Horizon-wide distances, no human story: this empty mirror-deep desert seems the perfect place to gaze into what I *am* before experience and definition, before thought and memory, story and explanation and all the rest. Here, I can simply *be* here mirror-deep without myself, empty as empty desert. I can simply *exist*. *Existence*, in and of itself: it feels like a kind of flight.

Cumulus

Vulture Wing-

Quaver Flight

Existence and *Being* refer to the primordial fabric of this shadowy Cosmos ablaze here with sunlight. But they conjure a world static and lifeless, even in their verbal forms: *to exist* and *to be*. Etymology, the archaeology of mind, reveals that if we trace those words back toward their sources in the primal word-hoard, back into strata beneath the cultural assumptions that shape our minds, they return to a living and dynamic nature. And there, existence comes alive. *To exist* traces back to the Indo-European root *sta*, meaning "to stand forth," and it gets there via the Latin *existere*: "emerge," "come into being," "become manifest." That is, "to occur." *To be* can be followed back through the Greek *phyein* (to bring forth, produce) to the Indo-European *bhu*, meaning "to grow, come to be." At a more primal level, then, *to be* means "to grow, to emerge perpetually into existence." Again, "to occur." And so, at the most elemental levels of mind, *existence* and *being* become the verbal *occurrence*.

Piñon Pine

Moth Flight

Mesa-Line Sky (Broken-

Basalt)

The conjugations of *to be* are etymologically distinct words: *are*, *am*, *is*. Traced back toward their earliest linguistic levels, they too bring existence to life. *Are*, for instance, can only be traced back through the Latin *oriri* to the Greek *ornysthai*, still far from the most primitive levels of human culture. But even in the Latin and Greek it is already full of life, for there it means "the coming out of stars," from which comes "to arise," "to come into existence," "to occur":

Raven-Flight

   Rain-Pocked Pumice-Dust

   Metalmark Light-Flick

Are shares its etymological root with *orient* ("east," "where the stars arise") and *origin*. So, at root strata in etymology's archaeology of mind, *desert rivers and mountains are* becomes *desert rivers and mountains orienting, origining*. And *we are* becomes *we orienting, origining*. *We* most accurately as the community of all things, all things perennially *origining* here: existence inside out all through and through origins.

   Rattle (Lightning) Snake

I keep stacking stones one by one into my own first-cairn, perfecting the least possible experience or definition or story. It's the simplest place in the world, this beginning, for the complications of memory and identity, thought and story and myth are perfectly absent. The cairn is made of ruins, this edge where the human is scattering into empty expanses of desert. It means everything around it, for where does it end? And it remains empty in a strange way, for its extent includes all of this desert stretching away, this wide-open topography. The cairn orients: *orient*, sharing its root in *oriri* with *are*. It orients, but says nothing—and so, celebrates things as they *are* in and of themselves, things *arising, occurring, origining.*

Ochre-Earth

Cottonwood Bark-

Parch Grays

Open-Blue (Rain-

Scent) Sun

Traced back into primal levels of culture, *am* is last visible in the Sanskrit *as* (*asti*), meaning to "live," "happen," "become," "belong," "dwell," or "occur." There, *I am* becomes *I belonging, I dwelling, I occurring*. The etymology of *is* leads to the same Sanskrit root as *am*, but it gets there via a different route through the Latin *esse*, root also for *essence*. *Desert is* therefore becomes *desert essencing: desert alive, belonging, dwelling, occurring*. And some say *is* comes from an Indo-European root *as*, meaning "to breathe." So, desert *essencing* is desert *breathing*, desert as breath-space: 冇.

Rain Pool-Ripple Light

Hawk (Red(Lit)Tail)

Etymologically then, *to exist* and *to be* becomes *to dwell* or *occur at orient, at origins*. This suggests that if we could look back beyond Indo-European roots, to the primal levels of culture where someone first piled stones into a cairn, we would find existence itself as all origin, a generative tissue in a perpetual process of emergence and transformation. This is the existence-tissue my ancient Taoist/Ch'an Buddhist teachers inhabited, the existence-tissue inscribed in the deep structure of classical Chinese and Hopi. And to simply *exist* here at origins, to *occur*, is to *orient* in the midst of shadowy Being ablaze with itself.

Being: there where the first cairn stood, *being* meant *orient-dwelling, origin-dwelling*. It's the dwelling those sage-ancients cultivated: ways *to be* at origins, to *dwell* here in this breath-space seed-time home.

Wolf Spider

Sky-Blue Sky (Lightning-Haunted)

Juniper Rock-

Root Gnarl

It was the moment when I first glimpsed what I *am* before the self-definition experience conjures: rain, which always seems a magical event in the desert. It was sometime around my twentieth year when I saw it: rain on pooled water, a few scattered drops, circles of light igniting on the dark surface, *occurring, origining*, then expanding and disappearing back into empty darkness. Darkness of the pool, but also darkness of empty mind's mirrored depths. I was just beginning to find my way, reading the ancients—Lao Tzu and Chuang Tzu, poets and Ch'an masters—but hadn't yet discovered Hsieh Ling-yün who, sixteen hundred years ago, at the very origins of Ch'an Buddhism, spoke of *empty-mind, a tranquil mirror all mystery and shadow.* And I had no idea I'd already answered the question Lao Tzu posed a thousand years before Hsieh Ling-yün:

> *Can you polish the dark-enigma mirror*
> *to a clarity beyond stain?*

No idea that in his epochal commentary to Lao Tzu's *Tao Te Ching,* Kuo Hsiang said of those lines: *Dark-enigma is the furthest depths of things. Here, Lao Tzu is saying that if you can polish away twisty thoughts and deceptions, then you can fathom the dark-enigma mirror's furthest depths.* Nevertheless, there it was: occurrence, sight, sincerity. And I couldn't find myself anywhere there! It felt like returning to home-ground I'd never known, like orienting.

> *Petroglyph Stillness*

> > *Vulture Wing-Stillness (Quavering)*

> *Sun-Still Distances*

It was the same with autumn rain in desert silence back then, a lifetime ago: a few scattered drops clattered in dry leaves, for a moment, and then stopped.

Occurring, appearing out of silence and then disappearing not only back into desert silence but also into empty mind's silent distances, vanishing right through me, no sign of myself anywhere. Vanishing through me like a lifetime.

Grama-Grass Seed-Floss Light-

Scythe (White)

Juniper Broken-Bleached

Dark pool, dry leaves—each raindrop orienting, opening this home-ground, this mirror-deep sincerity. It was from this magic of rain that the words first appeared: *From nowhere else, occurrence*. Those four words became a talisman that has stayed with me. *From nowhere else*: no desert separate from mind, no mind separate from desert. It's all sincerity: *whole, pure, one growth*. Rain clatters here in this nowhere-else. Lit circles ripple here. Sagebrush wind rustles, and memory. Thought rustles. Occurrence appears and then vanishes here—a lifetime vanishing moment by moment into this nowhere else, always opening a place for whatever occurs next:

Cholla Spine-Tangle Bloom

        Petroglyph (Wide-Eye) Gaze

Occurrence, occurrence: each fact is itself a place the eye perfects thanksgiving a little more, a little more.

        Raven Liquid-Light Wing

Sage (-Scent)Volcanic

Sight *is*, mind *is*: dwelling, occurring, orienting. From nowhere else. What is sight but occurrence gazing out at itself? And what are these thoughts but occurrence contemplating itself? Sight is a raindrop. Mind is a raindrop.

      Rain-Streak Skies

         Thistle-Poppy

    Sage Bark-Gnarl

Rock-Wren

And back then, a lifetime ago, gazing at the clean edge of high ridgeline etched against bottomless desert sky, I stumbled upon another Chinese insight: 直. I wouldn't learn about it for decades, but the pictograph portrays an eye with a line radiating out, and means "the eye seeing straight, or with direct immediacy." This ancient ideogram eventually evolved into 真, meaning "direct, real, actual, perfectly true, absolute." But invested with its full Taoist/Ch'an resonance, it means something more like "the wild thusness of things all clarity-absolute." Hence, absolute truth as "wild thusness itself." It's the insight of this cairn I'm building here, stone by stone. Gazing at that ridgeline, I oriented a little more, trusted myself to that wild thusness, that absolute clarity of things in the eye, in the eye.

Hawk Wing-

Flash Pulse

Mesa-Black (Broken)

Pulse

Pulse

Mirror-deep mind preceding definition, mind all sincerity: the ancient Ch'an master Way-Entire called that mind *a luminous mirror radiant with appearances*, and said: *Never leave this wild thusness of things all clarity-absolute, then you'll always have a place to dwell . . . If you don't inhabit all that, then what are you?* And he suggested a way into that dwelling: *This existence-tissue all thusness-clarity absolute—it has nothing to do with any name whatsoever.* And it's true. To see wholly, mirror-deep and sincere: to see is to forget the names of things. I forget and forget all the way back to that luminous mirror, my own name too forgotten. It's how we orient, how we become so much more than what we are. Dwelling here where I *am* what I *am*, it happens: *from nowhere else, occurrence:*

Lit-Lichen-Yellow

Desert-Distances

Anthill Rock-Grit

Sagebrush

明 combines two pictographic elements: sun + moon, their forms derived from the original oracle-bone images ☉ and ☽. Together in this ideogram full of still clarity, they mean "radiance" or "brilliance," and also "wisdom" or "enlightenment." It's true, light understands things with perfect clarity. And sight understands the way light understands, this solstice light all clarity brilliant everywhere, leaving nothing out, saying *Here! Here!* along the edge of broken basalt, tracing petroglyphs etched into burnt patina, hawk wing-ruffle, a single wandering light-line of sun-and-moon spire-grass, or:

Blue-Sky Blue

Ochre Pumice-Sand

Parch-Grass

We think ideas are how we orient ourselves in the world. And it's true in a way. But sight knowing things the way light knows, that radiant sun-and-moon *wisdom* and *enlightenment*: sight's clarity is itself the most primordially accurate and comprehensive idea. For if we trace *idea* back toward the primal word-hoard, we find its root in the pre-Socratic Greek: *idein*, meaning simultaneously "to see" and "the seen" in the direct physical sense of an object seen in the world. And *idein* comes from the Indo-European root *weid*, also meaning "to see." Ideas were the physical contents of sight, back then, not the abstract concepts they became as part of Greek philosophy's invention of mind as a transcendental entity. And *theory* too, sharing its root with *theater*, originates in seeing: *theoros*, formed from *thea* ("a view") + *horos* ("seeing"). It's like 𝆑, the eye seeing with direct immediacy, where *truth* is recognized as *the wild thusness of things*, things known the way light knows: naked truth, truth at its root as *aletheia*, "the disclosure or appearance of things," things origining, occurring, orienting. It's the truth a cairn masters utterly, cairn meaning everything beyond it. Wandering *idein* and *aletheia*, the eye's intricate clarities, I set out across the parched river-bed and onto a low mesa beyond, gaze back across at the ruins, my little scrap of a cairn. I continue along the mesa rim and eventually back to these ruins, where I coax a few more cairn-stones into place—orienting, orienting.

Pumice-Grit Wasp

Ink-Dark Lightning-Flash Sky

Even after a lifetime trying, it seems impossible to really fathom the elemental fact that this world is wide-open to me; and I am, I too am wide-open to it! What is this but the dragon-Cosmos gazing out at itself? The migration is late. Sandhill cranes pass, wave after wave flying low and chattering wildly, this world wide-open to itself in their eyes, too, their eyes radiant, intent. It's all sincerity—you, me, sandhill crane—*sincerity*, meaning at its etymological root "whole, pure, one growth." Dragon-mirror facing dragon-mirror: who could fathom the bottomless intimacy of gazing all the way into a sandhill crane's eyes, into your eyes, my eyes? *One growth.*

White-Scythe Seed-Floss

Raven (Krowck) Wing-Whoosh

Basalt Lightning-Sky

I can never take the world in enough, never hold it enough, caress it enough. I look and look, deeper and deeper. I listen and touch, taste and smell. But it's always slipping away, always eluding me. And I am, I too am always slipping away. In sight, things elude me perfectly as they become so much a part of me. It's exquisite and bewildering how all this eludes me in opening such vast distances through me: light-parched desert and this vanishing lifetime all flight, all death-flight breathtaking and wild.

Wren-Flutter

Juniper Pumice-Root

Mountains Blue-Distant

Emptiness: empty mind, empty sight, empty lifetime.
Without emptiness, where would all this vanishing
go, this vanishing that opens the exquisite possibility
of whatever occurs next:

Rain-Clatter

Piñon Cone

Ocotillo Bloom Sky-Tangles

To see is to forget the names of things, especially your
own. Where am I here, forgetting and forgetting all
the way back to Way-Entire's *luminous mirror radiant
with appearances*? I wander, gathering stones into a
cairn beginning to rise, to orient. I place nameless
ruin-stone carefully on ruin-stone, keeping things
whole. It isn't easy to know yourself. We're made of
so much elsewhere. I settle in here, gathering stones
into a cairn meaning everything around it, compos-
ing and celebrating all of that elsewhere. And as the

cairn slowly takes shape, I recognize myself more and more in all of that elsewhere, that *thusness all clarity-absolute*. It's exquisite. Sight mirror-deep, returning me to that part of myself I have lost: sight too is a cairn. Here at the edge of the human, forgetting and forgetting, I *orient*.

Fritillary

Cottonwood Leaf Light-

Tangle Flutter

Wasp-Flight

Orient, oriri, origin: the rising of stars. This is where the natural history of consciousness begins in the birth throes of this Cosmos, for the first appearance of stars opened space and light and the visible: the elemental dimensions of consciousness. After several star-generations, our planet was formed, cooling and evolving until eventually water appeared: hydrogen, created during the original cosmic expansion, combining with oxygen, an element forged in the explosive furnaces of dying stars. Water formed mirrored pools in hollows on the planet's primeval surface, and in these pools the Cosmos turned toward itself for the first time on this planet. It became "aware" of itself, "awakened" to itself in that mirrored opening deep as all space and light, deep as the visible itself. (The Sung Dynasty poet Yang Wan-li, whose poems keep returning to the magic of eye and sight as the gate to realization, said: *It's this lake's mind—that gaze holding the mountain utterly.*) Image-forming eyes evolved, and the Cosmos was awakened to itself once again, conjuring its vast dimensions inside us, creating the opening of consciousness, its empty and exquisite deep-sky depths, its breath-space. Sight, the eye: at the very heart of things is the eye. This primordial reality of sight survives in the oracle-bone ideogram for "eye," its steep angle evoking the eye as a wild and primal and creaturely phenomenon, a dragon eye: 𐤀.

Lichen (Orange

Blue-Green

Yellow

Red)

A first cairn, stones nestled atop one another— orient, orient. It makes sense that the earliest art forms would arise here too: petroglyphs scattered across this desert landscape, images chiseled into the burnt-ochre patina of boulders and cliffwalls: wanders and wave-forms, faces, sun and moon, bear prints and fish and bighorn sheep, spirals and snakes, sex and stars, stars appearing, orienting, shadowy starlit Being feeling itself, feeling and celebrating itself in wave-length festoon, wander-deep confetti. We assume that in chiseling animal figures into rock, artists were portraying objects outside of themselves in the world, much like an artist today would portray something like an antelope. But primitive artists were largely free of those assumptions. When they etched an antelope in rock, there were no boundaries between self and antelope, rock, landscape. Instead, they were acting at the origin-place where antelope and image share their source, where they were bringing that antelope into existence, creating the way the Cosmos creates: *origining*, *orienting*. What is it but the existence-tissue just learning how to recognize itself, how to celebrate itself, to orient?

Deadwood

Lizard Tail-Twist

Juniper / Piñon / Sage-Scent

This desert is all about boredom and loneliness. Boredom and loneliness, nothing at all happening, the least possible experience or definition or story: here I can feel the texture of existence itself, existence somehow open to itself in me. And more. The ancient Chinese word for this mirror-deep mind was originally a picture of the heart muscle, with its chambers at the locus of veins and arteries: 心. Hence: "heart-mind." And it's true: I *feel* each thing seen mirror-deep, each shape and texture and color an emotion perfectly unnamable and unidentifiable as mine. I must be so much more than what I am:

Thistle-Poppy Blossom (Rain-

Wet White)

There's nothing useful here. When we use things—technologies like tools and hearths and words—and they work, we don't notice them. We simply carry on. But when they break and stop working, when they fail, we suddenly see them in and of themselves: their sheer existence, thusness. Here, everything has failed. This entire village, everything people used to further their lives: it's all fallen into useless ruins. And for all practical human purposes, this desert too is utterly useless. Empty desert, empty ruins: this open emptiness erases all the meaning we want to invest in things, all the pattern and coherence, depth and purpose and value. It's exquisite how a place so empty and inhospitable could offer the possibility of *dwelling*. Here at the edge of the human, the world simply *is* what it *is*: *occurring, essencing, breathing*. And whatever I am prior to the usefulness of experience and definition, the meaningfulness that story conjures, that too simply *is* what it *is*—mirror-deep and *dwelling, occurring, orienting*.

Piñon Green-Jay (Blue)

Cloud (Basalt) Streaks

We inhabit a world of stories, and it is shelter like this village in ruins was once shelter. But there is no story in ruins, no story in desert emptiness. And it's only where story falters that I can orient and dwell. Only where story fails, leaving a scatter of words useless as village ruins and broken tools, perfectly useless and therefore revealing existence in and of itself, thusness, occurrence:

Piñon Root

Mesa-Line (Basalt

Broken-Tumbled)

Stories shape experience to define what we are, and there are no stories in mute-stone ruins. I keep walking out in different directions, looping wide and back— each wander a new view of that absence. I keep stacking stones. It's the least possible definition, tells no stories about me: sincerity, celebration-site meaning everything around it. I arrange stones one above two, two above one—the cairn now beginning to *orient*, to mean everything other than itself. It's an eye made of ruin-stone.

Desert-Scrawl Ridgeline

Rock-Chiseled Face

Ochre Sumac Berries

Who notices sight? Who notices dragon gazing out moment by moment at itself? But in that gaze, a celebration of occurrence vanishing inside me, I keep the empty distances that precede definition open:

empty distances of this desert, this lifetime vanished, this breath-space home. Today and long ago: they're indistinguishable in this mirrored gaze. Rain clatters here, for a moment, and then stops. Rain kindles pooled water, circles of light igniting on the dark surface, then expanding and rippling away through other circles back into empty darkness where new circles ignite. Occurrence. From nowhere else, occurrence: our breath-space seed-time home. From nowhere else, mirror-deep sight: dragon *ecstatic* here as me for a moment: *ekstasis*, *eksistence*, "to stand out beyond oneself." Dragon sees itself through me, for a moment, and then moves on without me.

Pooled Darkness

Lit Rain-Kindled Circles

There are many forms of shelter. A house provides shelter against wind and sun, heat and cold, rain and snow. Family and friends provide shelter from the blank exposure of loneliness. Language and story and idea provide shelter against the relentless immediacy of occurrence, against its arbitrariness and indifference and elemental meaninglessness. Self, too, is a form of shelter. It shelters the opening of consciousness from its own empty expanse, its elemental nature as the opening through which this dragon-Cosmos is aware of itself. And all of this shelter together defines the human. In shelter, there is no question of orienting. It's only when you leave shelter that the possibility of orienting arises. Wide-open distances, the least possible experience, the least definition: I wander light-drenched desert all mirrored sincerity, outside stretching away inside and inside outside. Here at the edge of the human, all the shelter of this village with its community and culture in ruins—here, I pile ruin-stones into a summer-solstice cairn already celebrating, already showing the way, orienting, orienting.

Juniper Gnarl-Light

Ochre Clay Rain-Pocked

From nowhere else, names occur: raindrops rippling this mirror of a world with vanishing circles of light:

Petroglyph Eye-

Gaze (Lit)

Swallowtail

The moment I name a thing, it's suddenly outside me, lost, sincerity lost. And names woven into thoughts and ideas: it's true they are the Cosmos contemplating itself, orienting itself; but in that contemplation, it is somehow distant from itself, lost to itself. How bewildering that distance, that loneliness. I wander here, desert and ruins polishing mind clear of all names, polishing sight until it's mirror-deep and looking out with the indifferent depths of the star-grained Cosmos itself. To see is to forget the names of things. It's disorienting, wandering here without names, without even my own name—looking, looking. Disorienting—and so, it orients. Gathering ruin-stones nameless into a cairn, sight mirror-deep, I know things the way things know me. I wander. It's all arrival, arrival, and it feels like home. I arrange stones slowly, one by one, perfecting forgetfulness. I give up a little more with each stone—names, ideas, memories— giving it all away, giving this whole vanishing lifetime away—orienting, orienting.

Vulture-Sky

Buffalo (Yellow Great-Blossom) Gourd

Mesa-Line Heat-Rippled

It's a primordial urge, the need to orient, to know where you are, where in relation to what matters: food, water, people, hearth-fire, home. This is the origin of that first cairn: people venturing further and further from home. And isn't it also the deep root of philosophy, and why ideas always fail? This need to orient, and the idea-tools it evolved in us: they were designed to work in the physical world, to help us succeed as a species. But suddenly, a few thousand years ago, we began using ideas to orient ourselves in abstract ways. There are answers to questions about physical orientation (where is home and hearth). So it seems there should be answers to abstract questions about the nature of things. But at its origins, *idea* is the Greek *idein*: "to see" and "the seen" together. We can only explain our way home with those primordial *ideas*, the ten thousand things of this world. It's in mirror-deep sight that we orient, that we dwell here in this breath-space home.

Wasp Veined-Wing

Rain (Basalt-Stained) Cloud

Rain Leaf-Clatter

This mirror-deep here, I am so much more than what I am. I think, and it is desert thinking. I hear, and it is desert listening. I touch, and it is desert feeling. I smell, and it is desert tracing scents. I taste, and it is desert's tongue. I see, and it is desert's gaze, wild desert gazing into wild desert:

Snow-Lit Peaks

Rock (Flecked) Wren

From nowhere else, breath. Life in, life out. This breath-space home simply *is*: *essencing*, *breathing*. Breath occurs, arising from nowhere and vanishing into nowhere. Desert occurs. Mountains occur. Sky occurs. Civilizations occur. These thoughts, these words. From nowhere else, sight occurs, this heartbeat occurs—this pulse, pulse, pulse occurs, and then stops. I add a few more stones to the cairn. Things seen elude me perfectly as they vanish inside me. They take flight that way. There's no difference now between a vanished lifetime and all these light-drenched desert distances. It's all flight, exquisite in its vanishing sincerity.

Basalt (Volcanic) Boulder-Scree

Sun-

Gnarled Root

Rock-Etched Spirals

Exploring the edge of the human here in these ruins, I stack stones, my little cairn nearing completion, *orienting*, meaning everything other than itself: desert, sky, the scrawl of mountain ridgelines. And sagebrush: *Artemisia*, from the Greek *artem*, meaning: "earring" or "to dangle." *Artemisia*, earrings dangling all blue-green-gray and sage-scent across the desert's empty distances, bejeweled distances wide-open who knows where inside me. Sight! That the world is open inside me! How marvelous: all day long, in its every shift of color or light, the world keeps me wide-open to it; and all day long, in my every glance or gaze, I keep this world wide-open to myself! All day long—the eye at the very heart of things. It's all *ekstasis*: this world and I together "standing out beyond ourselves."

Mesa Lightning-Line

Raven Wing-Tuck Flight-

Tumble

No thought any more me than a raven-cry, raven-cry vanishing through whatever it is I am. No thought, no memory any more me than whatever occurs next:

Desert Sun-Gust

(Rain-Clatter)

Basalt Stillness

Story faltering into word-scatter ruins opens me to horizon-wide desert sky gazing out at itself here through my eyes—orienting, orienting. The T'ang Dynasty poet Tu Mu, dismantling the mirror metaphor and even subjectivity itself in classic Ch'an fashion, described himself gazing *into a flawless mirror of sky*. And after all those centuries of vanished history, it's the same here. I don't know where sky is. Gazing into this flawless mirror of desert sky, I don't know where sky is. It is who I am.

Pulse

Sky-Pulse Distances

It's disorienting, that gaze. It's where old Tu Mu begins to orient in another poem, to find his way home:

日	暮	千	峯	裏
sun	setting	thousand	peaks	among

不	知	何	處	歸
not	know	what	place	return home

Sun setting among a thousand peaks,
I set out for home, no idea where.

And it's the same for me. Sun setting among a thousand peaks here, I *exist*: I *occurring*, I *belonging, dwelling.* I orienting, stars rising and rising at origins. Things keep vanishing everywhere inside me, eluding me perfectly. Sight: still no difference here between my vanished lifetime and these light-drenched desert distances. I desert, free of all that definition experience conjures. I desert wandering through desert. I desert looking out at itself through my eyes, thinking itself in my mind. I desert speaking in my voice whole and complete as silence. I *ekstasis, ekstasis.* It's where I set out for home, no idea where in this vast breath-space desert stretching away—sky, sky. It is all home.

Sagebrush (Leaves Earrings-

Dangling) Glisten-Distances

Seeing is forgetting the names of things. Here in this village of shelter now ruins, here in the desert expanses of this breath-space home, I sit with the world. Each word leaves everything else out: *basalt* and *cottonwood, mountain* and *hawk, occurrence* and *desert, cairn* and *myself.* No words anywhere, ruins, I sit with the wholeness of this world.

Juniper-Gnarl (Berries)

Rain-Streak Skies

Lightning

We can see through knowing to the question that remains: Being, shadowy Being ablaze with the coming out of stars: *oriri*, origin, orient. Stars drift light-years deep, ten thousand light-years deep in the eye, in the mind, the mirror-deep mind empty and orienting, orienting. Empty of all these explanations and stories, these ideas and words forgotten all the way back to those mirror-deep distances. Sight, sight: what can you do with so much emptiness? It's an onslaught, a lifetime vanishing moment by moment into me. There are no surfaces in a mirror. It is all depth, all appearance and forgetfulness and light-drenched clarity in flight. There is no mirror. No mirror and no mind.

Moth Buffeted-Wing

Sky-Stained Ridge-

Line (Snow) Peak-Lit

I desert, I settle a last few stones onto my little cairn empty and whole celebrating desert without all of these explanations, these words. Rock calendars announce solstice: light-line centers on spiral, petroglyph eyes ignite. The sun sets among a thousand peaks. Darkness begins to fall, and stars rise: *oriri*, orient, origin. I gather broken sagebrush branches—*earrings dangling!*—strip-off dry leaves for tinder, and sprinkle them into an airy pile on the cairn. I weave branches delicately above, then light the leaves. They smolder for a moment, smolder and then take. Tinder feeds the weave of deadwood, and flames rise celebrating all of this elsewhere I am, this occurrence, occurrence, flames seething wild and lashing orient, orient. This desert is a raindrop.

WALK TWO

(Seed-Time)

After retracing my summer walk across dry washes and uplands, this time with a dusting of snow melting on a warm winter day, I see it again: ruins sunlit beneath blue horizon-wide skies. There's almost nothing left of the village that once thrived here: a few remnant walls, carefully laid stone mostly tumbled back to earth. Almost nothing. Ruins are complicated, a weave of what is there and what is not there. They are a kind of healing, a return to something larger. Shelter, community, story, and all the rest—everything we are, everything that sustains us, all feathering away into so much beyond, so much elsewhere. It is earth's forgetfulness.

Scattered stone and stars: of the people who built all this shelter, of their culture and lifeways mostly mystery now, their loves and thoughts and the reasons they abandoned this place, what remains is mostly scattered stone and stars. Astronomy: walls and plazas oriented to the movements of sun and moon, seasons and stars; petroglyph calendars tracking those movements from solstice to solstice. It was orientation, and that too was shelter. Nothing much has changed since I was here for summer solstice. Now it is winter solstice, and I sit again among all this shelter in ruins, remains of walls once oriented to the sky. People knew belonging here in this village, family and community with its belonging-to-the-stars rituals, warmth and tenderness, and vast insight perhaps. But I haven't come for that lost world, its insight or mystery. And it's all too distant for grief, a thousand years gone and more. No, I've come for the vanishing, earth's forgetfulness feathering everything human steadily away into all of this desert beyond. You can glimpse dragon in moments of transformation, as it twists from one form into another. How beautiful dragon is here, how beautiful these ruins: walls of carefully laid stone mostly scattered back into desert—inside become outside, outside inside. Sincerity: *whole, pure, one growth.* How beautiful this sincerity-deep opening I am: sight where all of that elsewhere becomes everything I am, empty-mind inside become outside, outside inside. Sincerity, the disorientation of sincerity: Broad dry-wash between cliffs—sandstone, petroglyph-voiced. Expanses of *earrings-dangling* sagebrush and apache-plume. Sky and a few wind-ragged crows. Parched riverbed winding through, the wash opening away toward mesa-line horizons gone blue with desert distances, blue beneath sky-blue sky. Here in the ruins of orientation, I orient.

In shelter, there is no question of orienting. It's only when you leave shelter that the possibility of orienting arises, and these ruins are nothing if not shelter left behind. It is winter solstice, day long with darkness and all its clarities, ruins-moment where everything returns to rest, all occurrence death-drawn that it may begin again, that it may continue. I explore all this shelter in ruins, ruins and this ruins-moment when the old year dies away into the new, another form of dragon become visible: shadowy starlit Being all creation all destruction twisting through another transformation. Thought rustles, thought and memory defining that self I am, names defining what the world is, names and explanations, identity and story, all my carefully crafted orientation. Forgetfulness wears all that steadily away too. Here at the edge of the human, I sit amid ruins perfecting ruins, forgetting and forgetting until there's nothing left to forget, orienting.

This too is earth's forgetfulness, and it feels like flight, like dragon lifting away into flight.

This forgetfulness-ruins is the recluse-home my sage-ancient teachers inhabit. Dead now for centuries, for millennia, it's magic how their voices somehow survive all this forgetfulness unscathed, somehow remain alive in the silence of their books. They taught me all about this place. They left the gate wide-open, invited me in. And now I'm here with them, here with them.

Thoughts morphing one into the next and the next, moment by moment, tumbling and twisting: this too is dragon, a lifetime of dragon always in plain sight. We remember so little of what occurs with us. Perceptions, thoughts, experiences—they steadily vanish into us day after day, year in and year out, and we remember so little of it all. We are more forgetfulness than anything else, and yet all of that vanishing does not involve us in the least. There is no conscious effort, no act of will. It too is earth's forgetfulness. I give myself to that forgetfulness here, forgetting and forgetting until I am desert looking into desert:

Basalt (Snow-

Scent) Cliffs

Lizard (Open-Eye)

Village vanishing into ruins, into earth's forgetfulness: it is an opening. All of this elsewhere enters here, and ruins too become elsewhere. As I vanish, it's the same opening. I too become elsewhere. It's another moment when dragon twists into view. Forgetting until there's nothing left to forget, I find mind perfectly empty, sight alone remaining, sight wide-open and sincerity-deep: *whole, pure, one growth*. Dragon gazing into dragon. This gaze follows the ragged wall-edge horizon where ruins become that elsewhere of sky and desert stretching away, windblown textures of sight plundered by sunlight reaching these long-abandoned ruins, reaching whatever it is that sees. Call it earth turning toward itself in all its immaculate sincerity. Call it my original before-I-was-born face or mirror-deep sight, like my teachers. Or dragon. I dragon, I wander ruins perfecting ruins, gazing wide-open and mirror-deep until I am so much more than what I am: empty expanse of all this desert elsewhere, its sagebrush and juniper and ridgeline-scrawl distances. Here, no limit to what I am, I become myself.

Mesa-Line Horizons

Apache-Plume

Ferruginous Hawk

Light forgets it all perfectly, detail by detail, and with such exquisite clarity. It is my own forgetfulness. Empty and mirror-deep, sincerity-deep, I forget the way light forgets, and begin at the beginning—vast and deep, everything and everywhere.

It seems so ordinary, to look out across desert expanses. But it's inconceivable, isn't it? Who could ever understand it: to be the clarity of desert gazing out into itself, clarity of this dragon-tissue Cosmos gazing into itself? And what are these thoughts but that vast Cosmos contemplating itself? Language is the dragon-Cosmos confused and trying to orient itself. Meaning ripples through us, always evolving and transforming, nothing to do with us. It conjures thought and identity, idea and story like this. It is this dragon-Cosmos domesticating us, making a home in us, thinking itself through us. Etched onto desert rock, inscribed in books, voiced through air between us: meaning occurs, breathes and pulses through us, shape-shifting and forever on its way somewhere else, moving on without us, like anything else in this Cosmos: like weather, like continental drift or star generations. Meaning tries to orient itself, and fails, and moves on, leaving me to set out free of myself, nothing defining me, all flight here in this breath-space seed-time home.

I want to recognize myself, to understand myself. But meaning is not a separate realm, as we assume, a stable outside measure of existence. It is dragon's way of knowing itself—and so, is no different than any other meaningless ripple in the vast movement of this dragon-Cosmos: the twist of galaxies, the tectonic upthrust of desert mountain ranges, seasons. Meaning too is meaningless. The Cosmos shapes itself into desert basalt and cottonwood, into *earrings-dangling* sagebrush and mountain ridgeline, and they explain nothing, mean nothing. It shapes itself into language and thought and idea the same way, and they too explain nothing, mean nothing. Meaning is meaningless, is dragon tumbling all transformation further and further on—orienting, orienting.

Stories move horizontally through linear time, narrative time, shaping experience to define what we are.

But there are no stories in mute-stone ruins, and that transforms the metaphysics of linear time into the vertical depths of earth's ongoing emergence: 囲. Before I left here last summer, I scattered my little cairn of stone and ash back into ruins and desert. And wandering here again today, I begin to gather ruin-stones into a winter-solstice cairn—stones cold to the touch, rather than warm. Story faltering into word-scatter ruins, I begin to orient.

Feather

Rattlesnake

Vertebrae

This dragon-Cosmos gazing out sincerity-deep at itself, it is the same gaze whoever is looking: me or you, my ancient teachers or those vanished inhabitants of this village, earth's whole history of people, of sentient beings. It is dragon's history. And if it were visible, the history of that gaze, it might look like the depths I see mirrored in the dry riverbed below these ruins: riverbed rippled by so many feet beneath midday desert sun, it could be sand, or the river itself shimmering under a cool steady breeze.

I walk out across the dry riverbed, leave shimmering footprints rippled among footprints—orienting, orienting.

Whatever thirst draws me through.

Sincerity, sincerity: here in this breath-seed home, I gaze out through the eyes of my sage-ancient teachers, and they gaze out through mine. I speak in their voices, and they speak in mine. Chuang Tzu, for instance:

Live empty, perfectly empty.

Sage-masters always employ mind like a pure mirror: welcome nothing, refuse nothing,

reflect everything, hold nothing.

Here, walls wearing steadily away into desert, I forget the way things forget me. I see them mirror-deep, as they are in and of themselves, as they are without me. Clarity! Clarity! I continue on without myself. I shed histories, histories. I inhabit my absence, and orient, orient.

I speak in other voices. I speak in wingbeats, deep sky and peaks and rockfall clatter, chirps, trills, whirrs, speak creek tumbling over glacial till or stilled in pools, shrapnel cries. I speak always elsewhere. These words are my silence. Listen. Listen.

I ask only myself of myself. No answer.

Confucius says *language is itself insight*. Whorf the anthropologist discovered how true that can be in the Hopi, and it's certainly true of classical Chinese, with the 宇宙 cosmology inscribed in pictographic words and empty grammar and so much more. A dictionary must be the repository of a language's insight— and one day, wandering the dictionary I use most when translating, I came across the insight of classical Chinese distilled in this unattributed quote:

宇	宙	之	江	山	不	改
breath-space	seed-time	of	rivers	moun-tains	never	change

The rivers and mountains of this breath-space seed-time home never change.

His voice still alive in my voice here in this breath-seed home, old Chuang Tzu says: *I sit quietly and forget . . . I let the body fall away and the intellect fade. I throw out form, abandon understanding—and then move freely, blending away into the Great Transformation.* I'm beginning to see why he celebrates that as *tumbling and twirling through a blur of endings and beginnings . . . wandering boundless and free through the selfless unfolding of things.* Why he says *the realized remain selfless*, describing them as taking flight, as *mounting the source of heaven-and-earth and the ten thousand things in their vast transformations . . . traveling the inexhaustible, depending on nothing at all.* Kuo Hsiang in his commentary speaks of that *wandering boundless and free* as Chuang Tzu's "principle thought," as "the furthest depths of self-realization," and those depths of self-realization echoed down centuries at the heart of Ch'an, as in wild Cold Mountain's line: *wandering boundless and free and all delight.* Those sage-ancients wander with me here, as I wander boundless and free, never knowing whose journey it is. I stumble along in the details. I flow unscathed through every cell alive. I keep vanishing, keep opening a place for whatever occurs next. I never know whose journey it is. It is my journey.

So simply given in life: appearance, that unearthly clarity of earth, inexhaustible gift. Wandering the rivers and mountains of this breath-space seed-time home, I trust myself to appearance, that gift all transformation through and through. I trust myself to the way it vanishes sincerity-deep inside me, earth's traceless transformations unfurling through me instance after bright instance, eluding me as they return me to everything I am. *Whole, pure, one-growth* sincerity. It's all sincerity here in the ruins: not just sight, but the ten thousand things in constant transformation, too, appearing and disappearing perennially through one another as cycles of birth and death unfurl their generations, inside becoming outside and outside inside. Wandering boundless and free, I migrate on the winds of that sincerity, passing through generations, millennia, eons, glistening food-webs. I migrate through all my horizons. It's me. From home to home and back again home, I migrate. There is no limit to what I am, belonging so entirely to this dragon-Cosmos, this boundless tissue of transformation—not born out of it and returned to it in death, never out of it, totally unborn, unborn through and through. It is arrival. Empty and moving, I am always on my way somewhere else, always further and further into that arrival.

Thought-falling-silent ruins, old-age-and-death ruins, mirror-deep sincerity ruins: it's a place I can become so much more than what I am, traceless in the boundless transformation of things, dragon unborn and perfectly empty and always moving. The sage-ancients recognized those ruins as their recluse-home, and now I'm here with them. They speak in my voice here, and I speak in theirs. *If you aren't free of yourself*, Lao Tzu says in my voice, *how will you ever become yourself?*

Scatter is the nature of things. We try to defy that for a time with our meaning-making, our identities and storytelling: shelter, like these wind-scoured ruins. It's easy to take shelter for granted. Home, family, skin, language, identity, story: who quite notices shelter until it feathers away into a weave of ruins and beyond? And who could bear to be so much elsewhere always on its way elsewhere? Identity, story: it's too late for all that. I belong wholly to that existence-tissue all transformation pregnant through and through, and ruins are where I can watch that belonging resume. Death can't touch me here. I wander through the changing forms of my unborn identity here in this seed-time home, one form after another; and with each new form, I am more myself than ever. It's such wild freedom! I take shelter in house and family, skin-and-bone, word and selfhood. It works for a while. I take shelter in ocean and cocoon, gall and glacier, skin-and-bone again, and words, words and ideas and understanding. It works for awhile, but I am always moving inside out on and on. Sincerity. I take shelter in rivers and mountains, in feathers and wings, blue-sky shelter, night-and-day shelter, seasons, vulva, shelter in the unreachable structure of consciousness, in rain and sunlight, sleep and thought, erections, kitchen small-talk and soup simmering, stars-without-their-stories shelter, mountain peaks and thought and thought, heartbeat and sight, breath and thought and wide-open mirror-deep sight. Sincerity through and through, I am lost in all this shelter, lost and always on my way somewhere else, empty and still and riding the steady flood of it all.

My heartbeat sounds like dried grasses, like wingbeats and a sun-warmed stone midstream, like ruins-wind, hunger-stares, pulsar, pulsar, pulsar. Sounds somewhere else, sounds heartbeat, heartbeat like footfall, rainfall, silence, and shelling, shelling. Sounds tree-rings and cosmic background microwave radiation, wingbeat and snowmelt trickle-down ten-thousand-foot granite, silence, pulsar, dried grasses—my heartbeat, heartbeat, heartbeat, heartbeat.

I settle into stillness and absence, but they carry me further and further.

Desert too is unborn. But it isn't like me: its unborn nature isn't hidden by identity and memory, thought and story. It inhabits that nature wholly and always. I pile a few more ruin-stones into a cairn—orienting, orienting—cairn I will scatter away into desert when I leave.

Root-Gnarl Wind

Basalt Cliff-Tumbles

This dragon-Cosmos unfurls inexhaustibly through its vast transformations. It unfurls rife with creation and ravaged with destruction. We sometimes witness occurrence happening—raindrop light-burst on pooled water, wind-gust ruffling sagebrush, thoughts beginning and ending—but mostly we're caught in the middle of its unfolding so slow and steady it's invisible to us. Desert and mountain imperceptibly occur over millions of years. Sagebrush and juniper and ruins each occur over decades and centuries. How could it be so still and tranquil? These ruins, for instance, feathering away across centuries into desert and sky, scoured away by wind and rain, freeze and thaw, and growing more and more empty. It's the perfect place to get free of myself, to make something more of myself, something inexhaustible. Things mostly look like noun, but they're all verb. Unborn and dragon-whole, I'm somehow wide-open here in the midst of all this verb—I verb amid verb moving, moving. Here at the edge of the human, I wander with the tranquility of this vast dragon-deep Cosmos itself.

I am born of desert and sky. I soar desert and sky, feed on desert and sky, nest desert and sky, think desert and sky, bleed desert and sky. Extinction whorled in my featherlight bones, I am rooted in flight. I cannot say what words mean.

Desert gazing into my eyes fathoms all my secrets. Breezes touching my face fathom all my secrets. Sandstone cliffs echoing my voice fathom all my secrets. And vultures tracing the scent of my death, tasting my flesh—they too will fathom all my secrets.

Nothing holds still. The moon drifts blue sky above these ruins, moon immaculate, unscathed by the crowded millennia vanished between us: me, long-ago villagers here, sage-masters in ancient China. I depend, we all depend together now on nothing. Nothing holds still.

However perfectly I am known, the mystery remains. I am probed with radio-telescopes, evoked in poems, explained in encyclopedias, possessed in tourist photos, described with complex equations. And after all that, the mystery remains unscathed.

I belong, like this long-ago village community with its belonging-to-the-stars rituals, and there's comfort in that. But belonging too is empty, orientation empty. Where am I going, unborn and belonging so utterly to this dragon-Cosmos, its intricate weave of things breathing through their traceless transformations sincerity-deep in me here? It feels like flight, like dragon lifting away into flight, and empty, empty.

I am inside out all through and through chemistry: blood chemistry, geochemistry, neurochemistry, meaning-making chemistry, joy-and-grief-and-hope chemistry, memory chemistry, lust chemistry, spirit-aura chemistry, photoreceptor chemistry, nothing not chemistry blurring bonding scattering through photo-synthetic cells and bright puppy-eyes and solar-winds, through earth's traceless transformations inside out all through and through chemistry—empty and mean-ingless and moving, always moving.

Once blood is gone, there's nothing for the heart to do. It stops. It stops, and I set out on ahead, pulsing, pulsing.

An ache appears in the carbon cycle, in class struc-tures and the international order, pressure-gradient and fault-line, appears in neck and spreads to chest, ache in habitat and ecosystem and the distance an owl's voice carries through dreams of the deaf. Some-times it eases away. Sometimes it breaks free, and I'm on my way somewhere else.

I mark the way: earth cairn, sky cairn, fire cairn, water cairn. Instead of a subconscious, I have a river.

I find origins and extinctions, but I'm only passing through.

I am thrust up into peak-strewn ridgelines, tectonics glacier-scoured, veined with streams and rivers and fading to blue in the distance, where upslope winds carry me further, winged blue and further. I soar on those upslope winds, climbing from summer into winter, wingtip traversing rock and ice and cragged peaks skyward. I am carried on that wind, wings spread wide, wind lifting me as I migrate ridge-lines stretching away to the far end of sight, empty, empty-sky empty: I am rooted in flight.

I am what will come, will come. The inconceivable be-comes routine. My tears are blue from gazing into sky.

Looking out through this whole world of eyes, I am alone and moving. Woven into the web of life, tethered to the very source of earth's life-bringing change, I am alone and empty and moving. I never arrive. I keep moving, always moving. It is all arrival.

I keep forgetting what I want to say. There is no story in ruins.

I you, you I. Can you hear me? Listen, listen. It's me. I'm listening with your ears. I am as good a place as any to find yourself hiding yourself:

Juniper

> *Lizard (Heartbeat-Skin)*

Snowmelt Sun-Splinter

Unborn here in the Great Transformation, I begin at the beginning. I sit among ruins perfecting stillness, mind empty, orienting. Even stillness moves.

I heal the way I birth, from the inside out. Sincerity. *One-growth* sincerity. It is all healing.

I am winged sky and the talon-torn kill caught in open fields of snow, warm meat I tear from sinew and bone strip by strip, kill I leave among wing-prints when I flap away downslope into a fierce thermal, all sky again bearing taut, well-fed wings up into open sky.

Sheltered in these words cast against all this desert silence, I choose silence. Sheltered in these words cast against all this desert elsewhere, I choose elsewhere:

   Cottonwood Seed-Floss (White-

                              Lit Adrift)

I arrive home in that perfectly whole moment Ch'an masters inhabit, moment of primal plenitude and belonging, but it keeps moving. It's always like that: a vanished lifetime of moment after moment all plenitude and completion and moving, empty and incomplete and on their way always further and further beyond. I keep moving, always moving. My motion remains constant unless I am acted upon by a force. When a force acts upon me, it causes an acceleration ($a = \frac{F}{m}$) in the direction of that force. For my every action, there is an opposite and equal reaction. I keep moving, always moving further and further into everything I am.

I am blue heart-and-mind blue, indigo-bunting blue, blueberry blue, midnight blue, blue daughter-eyes blue, desert ridgeline-distances blue, sage-brush-green blue, bottomless-blue-skies-ahead blue.

Changing, I rest.

I migrate. I store up fat and set out from boreal forests to equatorial highlands, ford subarctic rivers, track magnetic fields down ocean currents, from the North Pacific to the Indian Ocean. I migrate root to branch to cloud, hillside to vernal pool. I migrate in flocks across wide-open mesas, migrate in families and tribes, schools and clans, pods and kettles (wind-drift, photo-period, electromagnetic field, circumpolar, solar-compass, irruption, vector navigation, coastal infrasound, ocean currents, star-compass, scent-compass). I migrate through all your horizons. I circle in thermals. It's me they are killing, me transconti-nental along the leading lines of cold fronts, of lake-shores and coastlines. It's me. I migrate circumpolar, migrate from seas to alpine streams, summer peaks to winter valleys, volcanic summits down to ocean beaches. I migrate into your mind, your dreams, your stories, migrate from one thought to the next and the next. But I'm only passing through on my way back to interglacial homelands, passing through generations, millennia, eons, through glistening food-webs (extinction, extinction, extinction). It's me, migrating through skin-and-bone, lives and deaths. From home to home and back again home, I migrate empty, empty.

What boundless good fortune, to be this form of all possible forms. And nothing holds still. What happens never happening enough, fact feeding wanting fact—occurrence scatters into its own directions. They are my directions. What boundless good fortune: form after form after form. I am whole, but never complete. I keep moving deeper and deeper through. It is all arrival.

I am somewhere near you, something quiet and beginning just now.

I am simply caught out in the beauty of $F = G \, \frac{m_1 m_2}{r^2}$, where F is gravitational force, G the gravitational constant, m mass, and r distance. Where F magically distills dead dust into starlight, fuels galaxies, shapes space and sets planetary orbits, bends light, invents the beauty of being simply caught out in it.

I die in many voices. I am what becomes of it all, and what becomes of that, and that.

I want to know myself, want to understand where these words are going, but I keep moving, moving. I want to understand this vast dragon-Cosmos all transformation, to hold it still for a moment in contemplation, but that contemplation too is dragon through and through. Perception, thought, insight: it's all transformation opening through transformation. Where am I going so empty and already on my way somewhere else?

I am rooted in flight. I breathe in sky, my lungs winged blue and bottomless. I have wings, always wings. I never go back.

I orient. I map ruins and find no end to ruins.

There are a hundred million missing women. There are blind eyes, muscle-starved legs, empty child-stomachs. I want to fill such absence, want at least to dwell in absence. But even absence keeps moving, moving.

White-haired descendent of nothing, I walk among ruins, tracing that weave of what is there and what is not there. I keep building those ruins into a cairn meaning everything other than itself. Here at the edge of the human—words wear away, flicker in and out of view:

desert

sagebrush

riverbed

sandstone

sky

ruins.

I hate it that things die, suffer and die as this dragon unfurls all creation all destruction through its unending transformations. Life ravels things into such miraculously intricate structures (rock wren with its delicate feathers and quick eyes, tiny beak and claw and synapse-lit mind), and how could such intricacy matter so little, how could it be so routinely torn apart and sent on its way to some other miraculously precise structure? It's all so empty, dragon tumbling on and on through aftermath, aftermath. And this dragon-Cosmos, this existence-tissue thusness: it's perfectly indifferent to all this destruction ravaging lives. Who could bear all that indifference? And I am unborn, gazing out with dragon's mirror-deep eyes, so I must share that indifference. I must. The ancients say that empty-mind all mirrored clarity is my original nature. But it isn't just *mind*, it's 心, pictographic image of the heart muscle, hence "heart-mind": empty mirror-mind woven through with a full heart. And I hate it that things die, no end to heartbreak. It's bewildering, bewildering to be this perfectly indifferent dragon-Cosmos feeling itself, thinking itself, loving and grieving itself. Emptiness. Who could bear it? No words, no words for the emptiness of tears blue as sky-blue sky.

I inhabit my absence.

I have lungs and veins of quartz. I have ions, thorns and ancestors, tools, glistening vulva. I have fruit, mitochondria, star-carbon and pollen, matted hair, blood, vomit, laughter. I have laughter, canyons, fire, feathers, death and sky. I have origins in the Triassic. I have memories, distances, enzymes, fins, fur, sediment, erections, wars, magnetic fields, hormones, hunger, have extinctions, words, antibodies, bark, hatred, chromosomes. I silence, bone, ash, have sight, beauty, mitosis, silica, food-chains and heartbeat, heartbeat, heartbeat. Rivers, grief, beach-glass, tongue, love, I have blowholes, continental-plates, strata and substrata, shadow, nests, touch, sinew, silence, breath, peaks, milk, migrations, gills, lichen, roots, talons, centrioles and spindles, red-shift, endorphins, flight, flight then and now and empty, empty.

I loosen the hiss and crackle of burnished curlicue seedpods, I wind-seared into the future spilling out seed.

And why hunger? It seems miraculous: consciousness, this opening in the opacity of things. We treasure it. But consciousness is utterly commonplace, a remarkably effective evolutionary strategy—and so distributed across a stunning range of organisms. It seems exquisite, each instance singular and miraculous, the very ground of identity and value and meaning—but set gravity loose amid the molecular actual, and consciousness won't be far behind: the inevitable result of gravity gathering interstellar dust into star and planet, planetary mud meeting lightning, then a few hundred million years of water and air and sunlight. No fundamental difference between dead matter and live matter. Consciousness as the elemental itself: heaven and earth, fire and water! So commonplace: how could it be treasurable? And doesn't hunger erase that treasure, reveal it as delusion? Predator and prey: things kill and eat each other without any compunction, no concern for individual identity or that miraculous depth of consciousness we most essentially are. It seems each individual identity is simply a fleeting form taken on by the whole fabric of earth's food-web: food-web all hunger, the steady transformation of fact feeding hungry fact. (Does it have to be this way? Why not a peaceful symbiotic system, like lichen, and have such possibilities evolved on other planets?) Why hunger—mineral identity feeding identity, consciousness feeding consciousness, hunger feeding hunger, eating, eating, that mineral sincerity: outside becoming inside, inside outside? But still, I love those beautiful depths of intelligence you see when you look into eyes, bottomless eyes: lover's eyes, stranger's eyes. Eyes of the hermit thrush I found in midwinter, so hungry it seemed to seek me out, stumbling toward me. I lifted it out of the snow and tried to warm it. And in spite of this heartless nature of things, this elemental sincerity, I was heartbroken when it died in my hands.

Ruins are aftermath: that murderous furnace at the heart of change laid quietly bare in the wind, and aftermath. Things get simple here. I am this empty opening where the dragon-Cosmos gazes out at itself, sincerity-deep, light-years deep. It's exquisite and terrifying: all this emptiness inside and out and moving. I gaze out from ruins across desert expanses, perfecting emptiness until I can't find whatever I am that dies. Dwelling nowhere, clinging to nothing, depending on nothing, I *wander without myself*, as Chuang Tzu says in my voice, *boundless and free through the selfless unfolding of things*, free even of death itself. Unborn, empty: what is there to die? When death comes, it comes as the Great Transformation simply unfurling its next possibility, carrying everything I am away, making me so much more than whatever it is I am now. It's exquisite and terrifying. It's a kind of flight. And because that Great Transformation is inexhaustible, I am in this flight inexhaustible and moving, unborn and empty and always moving on and on and clear-skies-ahead on.

I am the question desert poses, and I the answer. Mountains breathe my breaths. Sky thinks my thoughts.

It was wondrous enough when the birthplace of stars was mischievous Coyote scattering a bag of corn into the sky, as these long-vanished villagers may have thought, or Sun and Moon losing themselves in the dark love-making of solar eclipse. And it's more wondrous still that in empirical fact it is the love-making of all heaven and earth right here where heaven nestles down so caressingly close to these desert expanses. *Oriri*, origin, orient: birthplace of stars, but everything else, too, according to the ancients. For heaven and earth are the most magisterial manifestations of *yang* and *yin*, male and female, mingling always in a wild and boundless tangle of sex, and that love-making produces the perpetual transformation, the all-encompassing generative present that is this seed-time Cosmos: 甶. And however unlikely it may seem, it's true, isn't it? Sterile and empty on its own, heaven needs earth's generative power to create the possibility of life. And to engender the dynamic life of its seasons, earth needs heaven's infusion of energies: sunlight, rain, snow, air. This whole boundless cosmology of sex: heaven and earth are our primordial ancestors, so our own love-making must be the same. And with evening shadow rising out of the valleys, this solstice dark where the new year is birthed out of the old, you can see it: heaven tracing earth's dark body, caressing muscle and bone, every curve of her flesh, no limit to the dragon-haunted clitoral pool his tongue flutters at, diving, arching her back into the elemental heart of change, its empty genealogies all sincerity through and through. And no limit to heaven's distances where earth lingers tenderly, caressing their differing depths of shade, teasing them through her frail sacrificial boundaries, her traceless transformations. Heaven and earth *standing out beyond themselves*, igniting incandescent and wild *ekstasis, ekstasis!*

I feel dead if I'm not moving. I am hunger through and through. And never satisfied, I keep moving beyond myself, vanishing through earth's traceless transformations (*ekstasis!*). I am alive and empty and moving. Footsteps empty. Heartbeat empty. Breath empty. Thought-and-memory empty with the beauty of empty. Everything-I-am-and-ever-hope-to-be empty.

Empty-mind empty. Where-on-earth-am-I-going empty. Say it: *empty*. Even with espresso and dark chocolate, nothing not empty. Out of breath with empty. Living empty. Dying empty. Desert distances and rain and ruins, ruins empty. The Great-Transformation dragon empty with that same beauty of empty, empty and moving, always unfurling further and further through. Villages and cities are bombed into ruins, and I keep moving, moving. I accept with my whole body surrender and abandonment. There is no other choice. And what does it even mean, *empty, empty*

like flight, like wings lifting me into flight, and wild with that flight, why not say it: *Empty. Grain-of-salt empty.*

It's bewildering, all this emptiness. My ancient teachers spoke of *mountain-tiger-sky* emptiness: 虛, an amalgam of the pictograms for mountain (⟨pictogram⟩) and tiger (⟨pictogram⟩, deriving from early images like ⟨pictogram⟩). They spoke of *womb-labor-earth* emptiness: 空, combining the pictograms for "cave, the space under a roof of earth" (⟨pictogram⟩) and "work, labor" (⟨pictogram⟩, suggesting a process of generative emergence from an empty space, and later simplified to ꓕ). And so: heaven empty and earth empty. Heaven and earth in the *ekstasis* of their perennial love-making empty, empty. It's bewildering, all this emptiness whole and empty and opening me wild into flight.

The sun sets among a thousand peaks. Stone calendars come to life in last light: light-line centers in rock-etched spiral, petroglyph eyes ignite. They announce winter solstice, darkness where turning seasons end and begin again, this seed-time realm dying away into its own rebirth. Night comes, planetary shadow settling into ruins, and stars rise: *oriri*, origin, orient. Solstice: still-point open to planetary night. Nothing moves. I can almost hear it now, that evolutionary clock's chromosomal

tic

tic

tic,

three new amino acids every million years, three new mutations redefining species, adapting them to changing conditions—new possibilities against the darkness

of extinction, darkness of this year-end solstice night,
darkness winter stars drift light-years deep in the eye,
the mirror-deep eye.

I bow offering wing to wind, mountain to cloud, life
to death offering life I bow first and last offering rain's
drowse to the land, meat to beak, spring to summer. I
bow lichen to rock, gravity to space, vulva to tongue
and womb to child, earth to sky and sky to earth,
offering silence to silence I bow.

I exact each sight fathoming the eye's sincerity-deep
clarity, occurrence instance after vanishing instance,
each one another silent cry of the heart:

tic

tic

tic.

All that occurrence comes to rest here in this solstice dark. Nothing moves. Stars grain the darkness.
Nothing moves, then lost among sagebrush and
gathering solstice dark, desert-grass gold, the year's

final flicker flares where the ancestral ways continue
unchanged, and the heart's

tic

tic

tic.

Meaning meaningless as a raven taking flight: huge
black wings pulsing, pulsing. Meaninglessness my
winged meaning.

No words, no words for it all. Hungry for light here in
this solstice dark, I remember rain on pooled water,
a few scattered drops igniting on the dark surface.
Light! Occurrence! Hungry for light, I keep stacking
ruins into the simplest of cairns, a few tumbled wall-
stones on stones:

tic

tic

tic.

I'll scatter this cairn back into ruins soon enough, ruins scattering into desert. But for now, it seems perfect, seems complete and still and whole. We can see through knowing to the question that remains: Being, shadowy Being somehow ablaze with itself here, even after thinning and cooling for nearly fifteen billion years. Being all starlit shadow here in this solstice dark, *Being* meaning at root "orient-dwelling, origin-dwelling": I gaze into it, finding Hsieh Ling-yün's *empty-mind, a tranquil mirror all mystery and shadow.* I ask only myself of myself. No answer. No answer, and I'm already on my way somewhere else, empty and moving and starlit with *oriri*, origin, orient.

Planetary night deepens into this solstice dark, this hinge between dragon's destruction and creation. Everything returns to rest here, all occurrence death-drawn that it may begin again, that it may continue. Aging galaxies vanish and nothing moves. The ten thousand things crowding these passing seasons vanish. Cities, civilizations, whole ecosystems vanish without a trace here, empty. Everything returns to rest here in this ruins-moment. It's inexhaustible, this onslaught of occurrence vanishing into occurrence here, into forgetfulness whole. And I forget the same way, things vanishing relentlessly into me, slipping so

easily from memory: rattlesnake in shadow last summer, the ancient words with their timeless truths, the
unspeakable histories we must not forget, we must
not. Nothing moves here, where occurrence begins
and ends. It's home to all things, hermitage my sage-
ancient teachers inhabit. They left the gate wide-
open, invited me in—and now I'm here with them.
Listening to the shadow between each breath and the
next, I gaze out into this solstice night, perfecting a
place, a moment, until it is only shadow looking into
shadow. Empty, sincerity-deep, I open a place for the
stars. I orient.

To think is to confine yourself to a single thought. I
stop thinking.

The solstice moon drifts ruins low in its belly of dark,
pregnant dark harboring all my horizons. It returns
me to shadow, ancestral shadow all sincerity through
and through—moon, twice-sized setting moon, O
bright seed of darkness.

I unborn, dragon unborn through and through, I stay
woven. Dream basket, migration basket of horizons,

vessel of life unwoven, rewoven, shelter vessel: I stay woven.

I coax a few more stones onto the ruins-cairn. Moon's last light dies away into solstice night, the distinction between earth's dark and dark sky fading into one darkness. And I'm here, shadow gazing into shadow, as that ancestral patience to which all things return grows large enough it awaits nothing at all.

Ancestor sun empty. Life-force *ch'i* empty. Moon. Stars and desert ridgelines. Hawk, even exquisite hawk-flight, wings taut, circling up in winter thermals, empty. Oceans and continental drift, migrating caribou crossing rivers, cloud-drift, library shelves crowded with little packages of voice and story empty. Sage-ancients and their wisdom showing me the way empty. The way itself empty. Ruins empty. And whatever I wanted from it all empty. My small-mindedness and stumbling failures empty. Meaning empty. Meaninglessness empty. And dragon too empty. So why not say it: *empty, empty*? And no shelter, no shelter anywhere against this onslaught of transformation always empty through and through and moving, moving.

It's forgetfulness that lasts, flowing through its ageless clarity, canyoning that deep dwelling-place of darkness, darkness solstice night assumes in the eye, the mirror-deep eye. It's forgetfulness that lasts. It's a river flowing dragon-dark through its dark shadow, a place to drink. If you could look into the warm tissue that will dream even in my last sleep, probing every depth, you would find nothing but that same river, river rinsing through earth's frail sacrificial boundaries, its traceless transformations. Who knows what thirst draws me through.

This dragon-Cosmos gazing out sincerity-deep at itself, it is the same gaze whoever is looking. Gazing mirror-deep into early stars, I become my sage-ancient teachers gazing up mirror-deep into long-ago solstice skies, and those original villagers. They're long lost now in that river of forgetfulness, but I somehow look into solstice skies here with their eyes. How could we share the gaze of this vast dragon-Cosmos? How could all this emptiness be so warm and intimate and empty, empty?

I listen to desert wind: it is sky listening. I touch sun-warmed ruin-stone: it is sky's fingertips. I smell acrid-sweet sagebrush: it is sky tracing scents. I taste sandstone grit: it is sky's tongue. I gaze across ruins and out beyond to dawn horizon-light: it is sky's gaze.

My life, my death: they're perfectly transparent in things. I am made of distances:

Desert

                                      Dark

               Sagebrush

                                              Stars

     Ruins

Everything beyond words speaking in all its intricate languages: it is my voice. Footfall, crow-cry, sagebrush wind-rustle, and all the rest. And silence, mostly silence.

Here, in the still darkness of winter solstice, I inhabit the hinge of things. Everything is within reach—all heaven and earth stalled in their love-making—everything so close the slightest touch would start all that passion moving again, moving.

Emptiness grows so vast in this darkness that anything is possible. Hungry for light. Settling a few more stones onto the cairn, I gaze out, planetary shadow gazing into shadow. Stars drift light-years deep, ten thousand light-years deep in the eye, in the mind, the mirror-deep mind empty and orienting, orienting. Stars shimmer backache-shimmers. I can see through my death.

I am somewhere near you, something quiet and beginning just now.

Nothing exhales and inhales, blossoms out into a universe of stars and falls back into itself over and over. I take that breath, and give it away. It's me breathing, breathing empty and origin and *star-rising* orient, me

breathing out 宇宙, this breath-space seed-time home. Breathing out desert-grass gold, the new year's first flicker in solstice dark flaring. Occurrence, occurrence. Breathing out solstice sunrise lighting ruins that open out to mesa-line horizons gone blue with desert distances, blue beneath sky-blue sky (a few wind-ragged crows). It's me. I place stone atop stone and breathe, breathe, breathe. It keeps surprising me. Breath occurs, and I wonder how long such wonders could possibly go on. I take one breath after another, and another, thinking each miracle must surely be the last, each breath coming and going like another desert day swelling through me.

I desert, I settle a last few stones onto the cairn, then sprinkle sagebrush on top—dry feathery leaves for tinder beneath woven deadwood. I light the leaves, and they blaze up, flames seething wild and lashing, celebrating the new year's first sun rising. This desert is a raindrop

igniting!

I breathe it out, this light-burst desert. I breathe out occurrence, this dazzling sleight-of-hand dream scattering always into its own directions. And as it scatters, I scatter. I, dazzling sleight-of-hand, I scatter into my own directions—breathing home and seeding home and all orient, orient.

ABOUT THE AUTHOR

DAVID HINTON has published numerous books of poetry and essays and many translations of ancient Chinese poetry and philosophy that create contemporary works of compelling literary power that also convey the actual texture and density of the originals. These books are all informed by an abiding interest in deep ecological thinking, in exploring the weave of consciousness and landscape. This work has earned wide aclaim and many national awards, including a Guggenheim Fellowship and both of the major awards given for poetry translation in the United States: the Landon Translation Award (Academy of American Poets) and the PEN American Translation Award. Most recently, Hinton received a lifetime achievement award from the American Academy of Arts and Letters.